Five Great Piano Sonatas

"Pathétique" / "Moonlight" / "Waldstein"
"Appassionata" / "Les Adieux"

Ludwig van Beethoven

Edited by Heinrich Schenker

Introduction by Carl Schachter
Performance Notes by Anton Kuerti

DOVER PUBLICATIONS, INC.
Mineola, New York

Bibliographical Note

This Dover edition, first published in 1999, is a selection of five sonatas from *L. van Beethoven / Klaviersonaten / Nach den Autographen und Erstdrucken rekonstruiert von Heinrich Schenker*, originally published in four volumes by Universal-Edition A.G., Vienna and Leipzig, ca. 1923, and republished in two volumes by Dover, 1975, as *Ludwig van Beethoven / Complete Piano Sonatas*. In that edition, original footnotes had been translated and Schenker's preface retranslated.

Carl Schachter's introduction has been adapted from the original version written for the 1975 edition. Performance notes by Anton Kuerti have been specially written for the present edition.

International Standard Book Number: 0-486-40848-5

Manufactured in the United States of America
Dover Publications, Inc., 31 East 2nd Street, Mineola, N.Y. 11501

CONTENTS

PREFACE
To the Original Edition
[New English translation from the German text]

We know from Beethoven's letters and from other statements that he was not at all satisfied with the printing of his works. However, his disapproval and anger were of no use once the work had been printed. Moreover, the printing of subsequent works fared no better although he kept pointing out that his manner of notation was essential to the understanding of his musical ideas. The first editions fell short in that this connection between notation and musical ideas was not understood, both being entirely new.

Beethoven's notation always results from the particular character of the passage so that the notation of one passage is unsuitable for another. I referred to this in my annotated edition of Opus 101 as follows:

"In Beethoven's powerful and direct thinking tones are conceived, so to speak, as physical entities; this thinking produces for him a notation that is also perceptually convincing to the eye of the reader. The rising and falling of the lines—sometimes ascending from the lower to the upper stave, sometimes sinking from the upper to the lower. The deep significance of the beams—they convey to the eye the desire to connect or to separate. The mysterious eloquence of the slurs—sometimes they unite what belongs together or emphasize segments; sometimes they purposely contradict a connection in order to increase the desire for it, often counteracting each other simultaneously by their different time-spans. The upward or downward direction of the stems—they make us see the notes as actors in contrasting roles, clearly sketched in cooperation or counteraction; this is most beautiful when, for example, downward stemming foretells a long time ahead the counterplay of a group of notes that are stemmed up (or vice versa). The notation of the rests—they are omitted now and then in order to avoid emphasizing the coming and going of a part more than is necessary and in order to present the whole contrapuntal web to the reader's eye in a more transparent way."

Beethoven's notation alone can lead to an understanding of his musical ideas. Any alteration, be it made with the best intention, and especially in order to bring the musical thought closer to the public and to provide help for performance, tends rather to obstruct the access to Beethoven's compositional ideas and even makes the technique of playing more difficult! This includes standardizing the notation and attempting to "interpret" the text by means of so-called phrasing slurs and other aids intended to facilitate playing. A comparison of this edition with any other will prove the above assertion from bar to bar and from page to page.

Heinrich Schenker
Vienna
March 1934

INTRODUCTION
To the Dover Edition

For a hundred and fifty years the thirty-two piano sonatas of Beethoven have formed a cornerstone of the pianist's repertory. Although other composers—especially Haydn and Mozart—have written magnificent piano sonatas, the thirty-two of Beethoven surely contain the supreme examples of the classical solo sonata. One might imagine that works so universally loved and admired would always have been available in accurate and authoritative editions. As it happens, however, almost the very opposite is true. The edition reprinted here is the first that comes close to being an exemplary one. Not only is it a remarkable achievement in itself, but also it marks a watershed in music scholarship and editorial practice. The editor, Heinrich Schenker (1868–1935), is best known today as a music theorist whose contributions are generally regarded—even by those who do not subscribe to them—as among the most significant in the entire history of tonal music.[1]

Schenker, however, was much more than a theorist. To brilliant and original thinking his work unites scrupulous, painstaking scholarship and profound artistic vision. In other words Schenker's work brings together the activities usually carried on separately by theorists, musicologists and interpretative musicians. In uniting these activities (to the benefit of all of them), Schenker's work is unique in the history of musical scholarship and thought.

At the time this edition first appeared most pianists, teachers and students used one of a number of "practical" or "performing" editions whose editors thought nothing of changing or adding to the composer's marks for dynamics, phrasing, articulation, and indeed even the notes themselves if they felt impelled to do so. Some of these editions are still in print. Besides these corrupt texts two more serious editions were available, at least in libraries, but were much less widely used. These were the volumes of piano sonatas from the Beethoven *Gesamtausgabe* (published by Breitkopf and Härtel in the 1860's) and the so-called *Urtext* edition (also Breitkopf, 1898). Both have been reprinted and the latter is widely used today—indeed probably more widely used than when it was one of the only two editions that could be taken at all seriously. Although it is vastly superior to the "practical" editions its shortcomings are many, largely owing to the fact that the editor (Carl Krebs) did not use as sources more than a very few of the available autographs. . . .

Schenker's edition began to appear in single sonatas in the early 1920's; by 1923 the complete set was available in four volumes. Before producing this edition of all the sonatas, Schenker had brought out annotated editions (*Erläuterungsausgaben*) of four of the last five sonatas (Opp. 101, 109, 110 and 111). These appeared between 1913 (Op. 109) and 1920 (Op. 101) and contained exemplary reproductions of Beethoven's texts together with highly detailed commentaries including information on the source materials (autographs, first editions, corrected copies), interpretations of Beethoven's sketches where these were available, analyses of form and structure (the edition of Op. 101 contained Schenker's first published attempts at graphic analysis), suggestions for interpretation, and an exhaustive critique of other editions and of the important literature about each sonata. It would be safe to say that no masterpieces of music had ever received such detailed and loving treatment from an editor before; and indeed these annotated editions mark the beginning of much that is best in modern editorial practice.[2] Schenker was the first to make a truly critical edition and to develop and describe principles of editorship.

Perhaps the most important of these principles was to regard the autograph as the primary evidence of the composer's intention unless there were valid reasons to the contrary.[3] Schenker used more autographs as sources than had any previous editor of the sonatas, [including Op. 27 No. 2, Op. 57, and the first movement of Op. 81a. The autograph of Op. 13 has long since disappeared, and that of Op. 53 was unavailable to him] . . . Schenker also consulted first editions and copies corrected by Beethoven.

The way in which Schenker used this material set an entirely new trend. He was the first consciously to reproduce, as far as it is possible in print, the visual impression of the autograph. In other words he tried to be faithful not only to the contents of the works but also to the form in which the autograph presents them to the eye of the viewer. Very often Beethoven writes in a manner contrary to standard notational practice. Most editors before Schenker simply "corrected" these irregularities without realizing that they were possibly blocking access to an understanding of the composition. Conventionally, for example, the upper stave in piano music is mostly assigned to the right hand, and the lower to the left. How much more expressive is Beethoven's notation at the beginning of the last movement of Op. 27 No. 2, where the right-hand part emerges out of the lower stave into the light of day. This beautiful notation was not reproduced in earlier critical editions nor, indeed, in all later ones (for example, Artur Schnabel's). . . .

Another standard notational practice is stemming notes down in the upper part of the stave and up in the lower part. Beethoven sometimes writes his stems contrary to rule with great expressive effect . . . conveying an impression of orchestral writing. [In other instances, Beethoven does not use beams in the usual way; or will use slurs to emphasize the polyphonic character of a passage.] . . .

A problem of a different kind occurs at the second theme of the first movement of Op. 57, bars 35ff. The autograph survives but the notation of the slurs is inconsistent and in a way that does not suggest a purposeful variation. Here again the editor's musical insight must point the way to a solution. In the version that Schenker chooses, the first two tones (*C* and *E♭*) are slurred separately from the continuation of the melody. This highlights a significant aspect of the theme: that the opening upbeat consists of the same two tones as the end of the phrase (bar 39). Again this beautiful articulation occurs, as far as we know, in no other edition.

Another most unusual and valuable feature of this edition is the *fingerings*. It is not generally known that Schenker was a practical musician as well as a theorist and scholar; in his early years he was active as a composer and pianist. His personal copies of music abound with pencilled-in interpretation marks dealing with dynamics, agogics, rubato and (in piano music) fingerings, pedal and so forth. This edition, of course, contains no interpretative supplements to the score, for Schenker wished to avoid anything that would obscure Beethoven's text. However, the very detailed fingerings, properly understood, provide many clues to interpretation.

One might say that piano fingerings tend to follow one or another of two principles. The first is to make the passage as easy as possible technically; the second is to create a physical gesture that will help to achieve a desired musical result (e.g., shading, articulation or timing). These principles are not mutually exclusive. Most sensitive pianists will follow both in working out the fingerings for a composition, and fingerings of both types are found in this edition. However, too great a reliance on the first approach carries with it the danger of separating the execution of the notes from that of the interpretative nuances; shadings and articulations are superimposed by an act of will on a stereotyped and undifferentiated physical pattern. The most interesting of Schenker's fingerings are those of the second type—not just "basic" fingerings that "work" technically but ones that help to express compositional ideas in playing. There are more of these in Schenker's edition than in any other and a great deal of insight into the music can be gained from a thoughtful study of these fingerings. We shall point to a few of these arranged by category.

Motivic: Op. 81a, I, Introduction, bars 9–11 in the left hand. The basic "farewell" motive of a descending third is introduced in descending sequence in the bass. Schenker maintains a parallel fingering (3-4-5) for each statement of the figure and secures a legato by switching fingers on the same key. In the Allegro of the same movement, bars 39–41, the tenor part (left hand) plays a development of this same basic motive (*C–D–Eb–D–C*). Schenker's fingering (2-1-2-1-2) helps us to bring out the tenor part. The same motive (*Eb–D–C*) recurs in bars 48–49, l. h. (with chromatic passing tone), and in bar 61 in rhythmic diminution. Here again the fingerings help to project this figure. . . .

Silent change of finger on one key: The switching of fingers occurs mostly, of course, to secure legato. . . . In the Andante espressivo of Op. 81a, bar 15, however, the change from 1 to 2 is not only for legato but also to bring out the tension and release of the syncopated melodic line; the player ought to make the change at the middle of the bar so that he "feels" the suppressed beat. (The Henle edition, incidentally, has a single slur over the entire bar, a "modernizing" of Beethoven's notation that serves neither him nor the performer.) . . .

Pianistic: Schenker's fingerings are primarily intended to bring out musical ideas but many of them are also helpful technically. Among these are: his suggestion for the *Waldstein* trill (Op. 53, III, bars 485ff.); and the thirty-second-note passage for the left hand in Op. 57, II, bars 64–71. . . .

[The player should also be aware of fingerings designed to emphasize rhythmic and melodic groupings; suggestions for finger-sliding for various musical reasons; and of many of Schenker's fingerings designed to produce a desired articulation.]

In the fifty years since this edition first appeared its influence has been a powerful though not always a direct one. The great editors of recent years have learned much from Schenker and have followed many of his principles in their own work. That most musicians of any cultivation have abandoned the old "practical" editions is largely due—at least indirectly—to Schenker's influence. In recent years several new *Urtext* editions of the Beethoven sonatas have appeared, including a revision of Schenker's brought out by Universal-Edition, the original publisher. Some later editors have been able to consult material unavailable to Schenker (e.g., the autographs of Opp. 53, 79 and 90). But in most important respects Schenker's edition remains superior to any other, especially in the fingerings and in reproducing Beethoven's notation. In the Henle edition, for example, the notation slur-tie-slur 𝅘𝅥𝅘𝅥𝅘𝅥 has been changed to a single slur with an interior tie 𝅘𝅥𝅘𝅥𝅘𝅥, a change which in many cases alters the musical meaning (see comments on the fingering of Op. 81a, II, above).

This reprint makes available to a large circle of musicians and music lovers one of the greatest achievements of twentieth-century musical scholarship. At a time like the present, when performers, theorists and musicologists carry on their work in what seems to be increasing isolation, Schenker's edition has a symbolic as well as a practical value. Its study leads one to reflect on how necessary each of these activities is to the others, and how sterile—at least in a field like music—are the results of our present-day mania for specialization. The musician who uses this edition with thought and imagination will find his efforts well repaid, for it will help him to come closer to some of the greatest music ever written.

CARL SCHACHTER
New York
July 1974

[1]Schenker's *Five Graphic Music Analyses* (*Fünf Urlinie-Tafeln*) is available with a new introduction by Felix Salzer (New York: Dover Publications, 1969). Salzer's own *Structural Hearing* is based upon Schenker's approach (New York: Dover Publications, 1962). The only book-length work of Schenker's available in English is his *Harmony* (ed. Oswald Jonas, Chicago: University of Chicago Press, 1954). Translations of articles by Schenker have appeared in the *Journal of Music Theory* and *The Music Forum*.

[2]These annotated editions have not been translated into English. They have been reissued in revised form in the original German as *Beethoven, Die letzten Sonaten, Erläuterungsausgabe von Heinrich Schenker, herausgegeben von Oswald Jonas* (Vienna: Universal-Edition, 1971–72).

[3]Schenker was the first to emphasize the importance of autographs and was instrumental in the founding of the Photogramm-Archiv of the Austrian National Library, the first photocopy archive of musical autographs.

NOTE! *Throughout the book, the measure number appears at the <u>end</u> of the corresponding measure.*

Whether the five famous piano sonatas in this volume were given names because they are demonstrably superior to their 27 siblings, or whether they became so famous because they had picturesque names is an interesting question. Certainly they contain some of Beethoven's most impassioned and dramatic movements, and since these are the qualities he is universally most admired for, it is not surprising that they have become icons.

It is worth noting that three of these five renowned sonatas are in minor, while only six of the other 27 sonatas are in minor keys, demonstrating again a process of natural selection at work, favoring the earnest, stormy—even desperate—moods that the public associate so closely with Beethoven.

Passion and drama, however, are far from being the only characters Beethoven explored deeply: the tender, the heroic, the witty, the morose, the playful . . . these are just a few other examples of the kaleidoscopic variety of human emotions that he depicted so masterfully, and which are exquisitely in the foreground of many of the relatively neglected members of this unique set of 32 diverse creations.

These five famous sonatas (except the "Pathétique," Op. 13, written in 1798) were all composed during Beethoven's most fertile period, the first decade of the 19th century, which also saw the creation of the first six symphonies, the last three piano concerti, the violin concerto, the "Rasumovsky" quartets and ever so many other masterpieces. This was the composer's middle period, during which he perfected the style that brought him enormous celebrity.

It says much about Beethoven's character that despite its popularity, he abandoned this style after 1815 in order to forge a new, more enigmatic and profound one—that of his famous late works. It is this will to go beyond, to tackle the transcendental and to stretch his enormous powers and even risk shattering them in battle with the unattainable, that makes such a decisive difference in our view of Beethoven.

Had he stopped composing in 1815, the greatness and daring originality of his middle period would remain, but that extra dimension would be missing, the knowledge that this man was not searching for success but for an unreachable artistic truth. To this day, almost two centuries after they were created, his last works, like the Sphinx, retain a touch of the unfathomable that shrouds them in mystery and holds us in awe even when our understanding falls short. In them Beethoven had forged a new style which revolutionized music.

Heinrich Schenker's classic edition of the Beethoven sonatas, from which the contents of this volume are extracted, remains, in this age of growing interest in so-called "Urtext" editions, a trustworthy, authentic source. Indeed, it was the first widely available edition that attempted to reproduce as faithfully as possible the uncontaminated intentions of the composer. The only editorial additions are the fingerings, which should help the less advanced student, yet can easily be ignored by the more advanced. The pedal markings on the other hand are all by Beethoven; he used them only to indicate a few radical, unusual pedal effects, and certainly assumed that players would use their own taste and musicality in applying the pedal judiciously—and copiously—elsewhere.

There is no edition, to this day, that correctly differentiates between the various articulation marks that Beethoven used to denote shortness (and in many instances, probably emphasis as well). Beethoven himself, in a letter, insisted that the difference between "strokes" (wedge-shaped marks)

"Waldstein" Sonata: I, mm. 32–3

and dots was of great importance. In truth, it would be a nigh impossible task to properly distinguish the strokes from the dots, because Beethoven was so messy and inconsistent in his indications. Dots often gradually metamorphize into strokes and vice versa, in the course of the same passage.

Schenker chose to use mainly strokes, which is a reasonable solution, inasmuch as the manuscripts indeed have far more unambiguous strokes than dots. The only exception is in the *portato* markings,[1] which both in the manuscripts and in this edition always have clearly recognizable dots under the slurs.

It is important not to erroneously assume that strokes indicate extreme shortness (staccatissimo) or sharp accentuation. Indeed, there is much evidence to indicate that Beethoven's strokes (which in the manuscripts are not wedge-shaped but simply vertical or slanted lines) were meant to be longer than staccato dots, though some older authorities maintain the opposite. In any event, a broad range of lengths should be employed by the performer, corresponding to the desired character of the music.

The 32 sonatas are a never-ending joy and inspiration to both amateur and professional musicians. An undisputed cornerstone of the pianist's repertoire, they overflow with individuality and variety. It can fairly be asserted that no two of them are even similar to each other. They are a unique testimonial to the heroic personalization of music that was Beethoven's triumph, and to his unending search for both logical coherence and improvisatory spontaneity. Their influence on Beethoven's contemporaries and on later composers and performers is incalculable.

SONATA NO. 8 IN C MINOR, OP. 13 ("Pathétique")

The grandeur of the "Pathétique" Sonata[2] is immediately clear from the fact that it starts with a slow introduction. While earlier composers often did this in symphonic works, it was rare to do so in a mere instrumental sonata. But one must question whether this opening is really an introduction at all, for it recurs at the beginning of the development (bar 137) and in the coda (bar 295),[3] and material from it is used in the development. Is this arresting start not rather an integral part of a unique, original form?

The manuscript is lost, and the available sources leave some doubt as to whether the exposition should be repeated from the very beginning, or just from the start of the *Allegro molto e con brio* (bar 11). The last passage of the exposition (bar 125) seems to cry out for a return to the forceful, solemn opening chords, for the analogous passages (prior to the second ending, and at bar 289) do indeed lead to the material of the introduction, not to the impatient, nervous darting of the Allegro theme.

Rarely has so much been said so powerfully, simply and briefly as in the second movement, *Adagio cantabile;* its perfect proportions and deep emotions seem to suspend time, giving it a vast and warmly spacious aura. The second episode (bar 37) comes unexpectedly and hauntingly in the tonic minor, and reveals almost more the character of a development than of an episode. Touching and superb is how the new triplet motion accompaniment introduced in this episode is adopted in the final return of the main theme (bar 51). During the episode these triplets had created anxiety but now, returned to the familiar surroundings and major key of the main theme, they intensify the theme's warmth and depth, giving the movement a wondrously wholesome unity.

The Rondo finale is less intense than the other movements; indeed, it would have been futile to compete with the dramatic intensity of the first movement, while to write a humorous or brilliant rondo, especially in the absence of a menuetto, would disturb the sublime effect of the *Adagio cantabile* movement. The Rondo's cool, lyrical poignancy—which only occasionally echoes some of the first movement's storminess—gives the "Pathétique" an exquisite balance of moods.

SONATA NO. 14 IN C-SHARP MINOR, OP. 27, NO. 2 (*Sonata quasi una Fantasia*) ("Moonlight")

Why has the first movement of the so-called "Moonlight" Sonata become so notorious? One of Beethoven's most abstract creations, gathering force from its texture and its subtle yet powerful harmonic processes, it is hardly the sort of music one would expect to top the charts. Perhaps its success is partly attributable to the excellent public relations promoted by its spurious title.[4] The sonata is certainly one of Beethoven's most original and inspired creations, spanning a wide range of emotions from the hypnotic, solemn lament of the first movement, to the tragic and overpowering passion of the last. However, the very fame and commercial degradation of the opening *Adagio sostenuto* has perhaps deprived the work to some extent of its rightful place in the concert hall, just because it has been so exploited and rendered almost unrecognizable by over-dramatized, over-romanticized performances. As a result, the performer who plays this movement authentically risks being accused of understatement; still, its greatest effect comes when performed with the utmost subtlety and restraint. Beethoven himself wrote that "the entire Adagio is to be played with the utmost delicacy" and marked most of it **pp**.

Most performers overdot the rhythm of the theme, which can make it sound rather military and clipped; on the other hand, it is not easy to play the rhythm precisely (the 16th note coming very soon after the third triplet) without sounding academic and artificial.

The second movement is the shortest possible menuetto, gracious and fragile. Its effect is magnified by its position between the two overpowering outer movements—Liszt called it "a flower between two abysses."

The finale, *Presto agitato,* is one of Beethoven's most intense and violent outbursts, full of merciless shocks, roaring sonorities and pleading melodies. It is in sonata form, and if we try to imagine it cast as a rondo, we can sense the necessity of using the more dramatic form for such angry contents.

The breathless second theme (bar 21) dominates the development, and its effect is exquisitely magnified and darkened when it is transferred from the treble to the bass (bar 75). The unrelieved odor of minor wafts throughout the movement, except for one moment when the second theme briefly touches major (bar 79). A bitter and spectacular cadenza (bar 177) crystallizes the desperate character of the entire piece to close off this masterwork majestically.

SONATA NO. 21 IN C MAJOR, OP. 53 ("Waldstein")

Judging from his frugality here in the use of themes, Beethoven would have fit in well with those American pioneers whose motto (now adopted by environmentalists) was "use it up, wear it out, do without." If earlier he came close to "wearing out" his ideas by avidly developing and exploiting them, in the "Waldstein" Sonata he comes about as close as one can to "doing without." The only full-fledged melody that could stand on its own in the entire piece is the serene and delicate Rondo theme.

Beethoven was already known for his bold harmonic contrasts, but they become even more abrupt and fascinating in this work; in rapid succession the opening *Allegro con brio* touches B-flat major, D minor, F minor, and B major before finally alighting, unconventionally, on E major for the second subject (bar 35). This theme is a sort of melody, but seen in isolation it is a pallid one of rather square dimensions. Luckily, like an exquisite woman, it need say nothing; it suffices for it to shine forth in its exotic E-major coloring.

Beethoven's range of purely pianistic color is increased in the "Waldstein," for he experiments with many different ways of creating textures, including the unusual use of repeated chords and tremolandos; recklessly leaping broken octaves; shimmering octave glissandos; extravagant pedal effects; and the almost obsessive use of trills.

But color alone cannot fully satisfy, just as even the most exquisitely prepared spices and sauces do not constitute a meal. Filling the gap are the newly emancipated accompaniments, which have risen up, overthrown the oppressive aristocracy of melody and decided they can get along quite well enough by themselves. If the slave can become the master, and the medium can become the message, cannot the accompaniment become the theme?

What are the opening repeated chords (note, by the way, that there are no staccato marks over these) if not an accompaniment in search of a tune? Filling it out are flying wisps of motives peeking out from various registers. That Beethoven fashioned such a majestic movement almost exclusively from such scraps is quite miraculous.

The slow movement is clearly in Beethoven's improvisatory style, focusing almost exclusively on the development of the opening ascending motive. Like many of the middle-period slow movements, it serves more as an introduction to the finale than as a full movement in its own right.

The last movement starts with such a fond, hazy intimacy, that one fully expects a *grazioso*-type rondo. The prescribed pace is leisurely, the dimensions are extremely spacious—one senses no desire to leave the sweet serenity of the listless tune. But a trill, seemingly started for the pure joy of its delicate sonority, unexpectedly turns into an alarm bell that summons forth a stunning reappearance of the erstwhile timid theme in full battle dress, and leads us into a heroic bravura movement.

Radical pedal effects are marked consistently and carefully throughout; the pedal is to be held down for up to 15 measures, melting together tonic and dominant, major and minor, and contradicting rests and staccatos. While the piano's sustaining power has greatly increased since Beethoven's time, it is obvious that even on his instrument these markings would have produced clashes; a special surrealistic effect was certainly intended.

In a maneuver typical of Beethoven, the coda (bar 403) precipitously lurches us out of the sedate tempo into a spectacular final chase in which the rondo theme is heard almost four times as rapidly as in its previous incarnation. It thus acquires a tingling energy, remotely suggestive of a hot jazz beat, which drives the work to a dazzling conclusion.[5]

SONATA NO. 23 IN F MINOR, OP. 57 ("Appassionata")

The "Appassionata" finds Beethoven at the height of his dramatic power. Each movement has an ecstatic climax near its end, rather than at the recapitulation. In the first movement the climax is breathless and overpowering (bar 256); in the second it is of great expressive warmth and yearning (bar 79); and in the finale it is utterly possessed with demonic furor (bar 341).

The soft, distant opening of the first movement casts a majestic and foreboding mood that is amplified by the lonely sonority of its naked arpeggio figure. An ominous, deep motive (bar 10), rhythmically identical to the famous motive of the 5th Symphony (written about two years later), takes over and quickly leads to the first of the sonata's many explosive eruptions. The shining second theme (bar 35) adopts the same nervous rhythm and a very similar arpeggio figure as that of the main theme, thus providing an unusual sense of unity. How wondrous that the composer could establish such diverse moods with the same material, and especially that he could create such a warm, noble tranquility with such a bumpy rhythm.

This warmth rapidly expires, and the rest of the exposition is filled with furor and despair, mostly in the distant key of A-flat minor—whence it would be difficult to return directly to F minor for the customary repeat. In any event, the exposition is so full of arresting dramatic omens that repeating them would sound phony. This is, in fact, Beethoven's first full-scale opening movement in sonata form that does not repeat the exposition.

A similar consideration applies to the recapitulation (bar 135), which would sound academic if it were identical to the opening. Just as we are transformed by the sonata's events, the music itself can hardly remain aloof and untouched. Indeed, it becomes far more urgent, mainly due to the new pulsating accompaniment deep in the bass.

After some stupendous virtuoso passages the music of the first movement finally exhausts itself, winding down with reverberations of the repeated-note motive, until the coda precipitously redoubles its energy and pulse (bar 238). What makes it so agonizing is not only the increased tempo and the battle between the pianist and the piano, but the fact that the movement's one friendly and serene element—the second subject—is now used in minor, its character shockingly altered: the only wisp of sunlight has been eclipsed and banished.

The second movement is a set of variations whose theme is no more than a stately, nobly expressed harmonic pattern. Each of the three variations doubles the motion of its predecessor, but only in the last (bar 49) does Beethoven abandon the reserved, sweetly introspective mood and break into an urgently expressive one. After a repeat of the theme, made to sound like a fading memory by continually shifting from one octave to another (bar 81), the music halts on a very silent but threatening diminished chord (bar 96), which is then attacked, repeatedly and mercilessly, leading us into the finale.

Here, as in the "Waldstein" Sonata, the accompaniment is the very essence of the music; its *perpetuum mobile* pervades all. It is quiet but chilling, like the swells in the middle of the ocean. The *Allegro ma non troppo* marking should be taken seriously, so that the figure can be profoundly melodic and not sound like a hasty, unimportant wash. Over it rises a series of desolate, penetrating cries, separated by gasp-like rests (bar 38 *et al.*)[6] The finale is in sonata form, but instead of the usual repetition of the exposition (which, as noted, was omitted in the first movement) Beethoven asks, most unconventionally, for the repeat of the combined development and recapitulation. This unique scheme prolongs the movement beyond expectation, while the accompaniment continues to trickle on, accumulating more and more energy.

As it winds on, the tension climbs steeply like water building up behind a dam that must eventually burst. And burst it does, breaking into a dance that is both demonic and majestic (bar 308); at last the accompanying material, which for an unbearably long and tense expanse had been held so tightly reined-in, is allowed to cascade out tumultuously, sweeping us to a frenetic conclusion.

SONATA NO. 26 IN E-FLAT MAJOR, OP. 81A ("Les Adieux")

Op. 81a stands as the last of the famous middle-period sonatas, and could be seen as this group's culmination point, in which the finest balance of content is achieved. Compared to Opp. 53 and 57, it is shorter but appears just as substantial due to its concentrated expressive quality; pianistically slightly less virtuosic, it is still able to dazzle without distracting from the emotional content; only slightly less economical in its use of material, it appears far more generous due to the less fragmented and warmer character of its ideas.

Above the three thoughtfully descending opening chords, Beethoven inscribed the German words "Lebe wohl" (Fare thee well). Much to the composer's annoyance, the publisher arbitrarily attached the French translation "Les Adieux" to the title page, and this has remained with the work ever since.

Only in two or three other works does Beethoven indicate a program content for his music, but the program of "Les Adieux" does not evoke images like the thunderstorm, the peasant dance, or the cuckoo found in the 6th Symphony. Rather, it expresses three distinct moods: Beethoven's grief at bidding farewell to the Archduke Rudolph, his friend and patron;[7] his loneliness during the Archduke's absence (second movement); and his joy upon the friend's safe return (last movement).

A few passages could be interpreted more concretely: the opening motive might represent the distant posthorns of the stagecoach carrying the Archduke away; the Allegro theme (bar 17) sounds like the two friends being forcibly and painfully pulled apart; the isolated and unaccompanied passages of 32nd notes in the Andante (second movement, bar 13) must be a symbolic representation of loneliness; and the explosive outburst at the beginning of the last movement suggests Beethoven's having unexpectedly caught sight of the returning Archduke, and the two friends scurrying to embrace each other, followed by a dance of rejoicing.

To return to the first movement, the Adagio introduction immediately sets the serious mood of the work. The unexpected minor mode of the third "Lebe wohl" chord is the first in a series of haunting harmonic effects; when the "Lebe wohl" motive is repeated, the third chord is not just unexpected, it is almost erotically shocking as it melts into the distant key of C-flat major (bar 8).

Startling harmonizations of the third note of the "Lebe wohl" motive abound in the short development, and in the coda. These three descending notes also form the second theme (bar 50), and just before the end of the movement they reappear (bars 231ff) in an echo effect, which is remarkable for the simultaneous striking of the tonic and dominant chords.

The profoundly melancholy second movement, like so many slow movements of this period, is on the borderline between being autonomous and serving as an introduction to the last movement. Its most poignant moments occur where the music becomes infinitely sweet in the midst of the general sadness, perhaps a stirring memory of earlier happiness.

The rollicking finale displays its exhilaration uninterruptedly until the coda (bar 176), where the principal theme is developed in a reflective mood and at a slower tempo, possibly representing a momentary remembrance of the painful absence.

While all these extra-musical allusions may fit perfectly and help our enjoyment of the music, what really matters are not the events, but the universal emotions associated with them.

ANTON KUERTI
Toronto
Summer 1999

Austro-Canadian pianist Anton Kuerti is considered among the world's foremost Beethoven interpreters. He has played with most of the leading orchestras of North America, and has recorded and performed all the Beethoven sonatas and concerti.

FOOTNOTES

[1]*Portato* is one of the most widely misunderstood indications in Beethoven's music. Generally, *portato* notes should be as long as possible without actually overlapping; in the case of repeated notes or chords, they may even be connected with pedal.

[2]"One day this author heard the master lament that he had ever added the designation *pathétique* to the opus 13 sonata. 'The whole world,' he complained, 'seizes upon a single sonata because it has a name that the pianists can exploit.' Music dealers say that while piano music in general is now in greater demand, the *Sonate pathétique* sells more copies than any other piece. No wonder a German publisher once told the composer that he would pay ten thousand gulden for a new *Sonate pathétique*! Such is the strength of a foreign word whose meaning remains unknown to the majority of the piano-playing public! How often Beethoven would have had to append the designation *pathétique* to every kind of composition if he had wanted to be consistent!"
Anton Felix Schindler
Beethoven As I Knew Him (1860)

[3]Let us not forget that Schenker's bar numbers always appear at the *end* of the corresponding measure—a sometimes confusing but always consistent feature of his edition.

[4]The name has been attributed to a review written by poet and critic Heinrich Rellstab, likening the motion of the first movement to a boat floating by moonlight on Lake Lucerne.

[5]*Note:* A hint for the execution of the famous octave glissandos bars 465–474: Have a piano technician make sure that the front rail bushings are well lubricated so the keys can glide down smoothly even under intense lateral pressure.

[6]It is best not to hold the pedal through these poignant pauses.

[7]On April 9, 1809, Austria declared war on France. By mid-May, following a bombardment of the Austrian capital, Vienna was in French hands. It was during this period of danger that Rudolph left the besieged city.

Five Great Piano Sonatas

"Pathétique" / "Moonlight" / "Waldstein"
"Appassionata" / "Les Adieux"

SONATE. (PATHÉTIQUE.)
Op. 13.

Dem Fürsten Carl von Lichnowsky gewidmet.

8.

Attacca subito l' Allegro:

1) Three triplets. 2) Here 6 = 3 x 2. 3) Here 6 = 2 x 3.

2

Allegro molto e con brio.

1) Short appoggiatura.

Adagio cantabile.

RONDO.
Allegro.

1) [symbol] 2) Short appoggiatura.

18

SONATE.

Op.27. Nº 2.
(Sonata quasi una Fantasia.)

Der Gräfin Julie Guicciardi gewidmet.

Adagio sostenuto.

Si deve suonare tutto questo pezzo delicatissimamente e senza sordini.

1) The pedal indications are Beethoven's.

22

Attacca subito il seguente.

Presto agitato.

SONATE.

Op. 53.

Dem Grafen von Waldstein gewidmet.

Allegro con brio.

1) The fingering in italics and the pedal indications are Beethoven's.

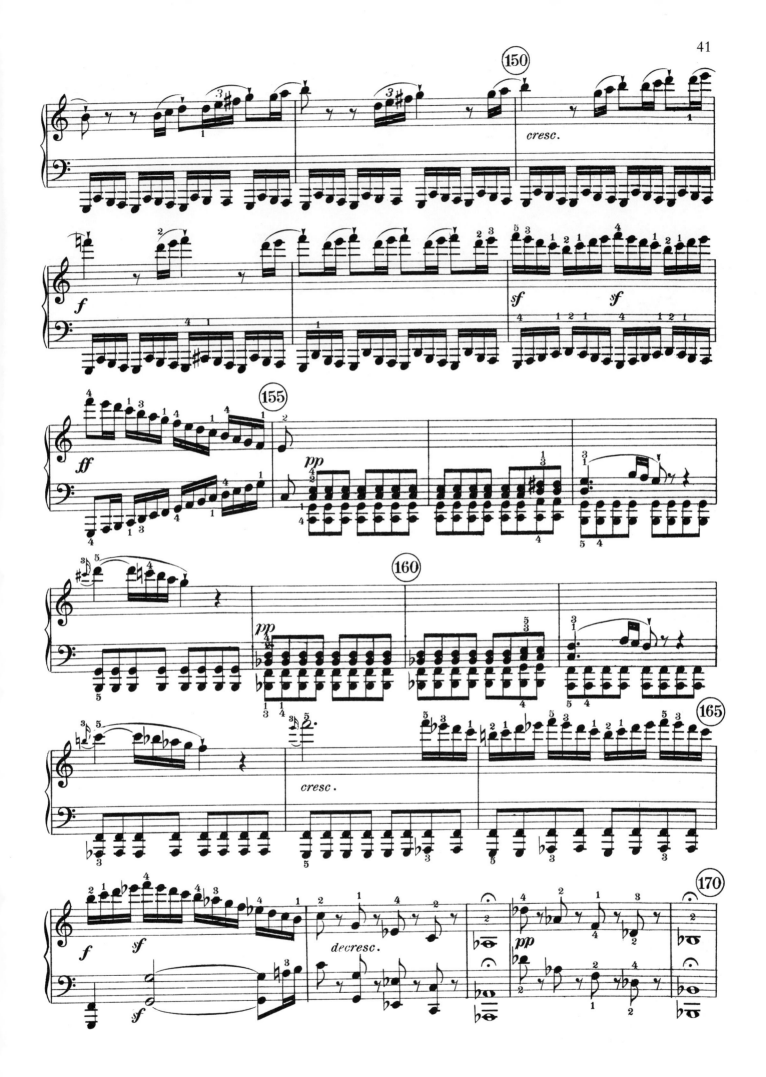

1) The original edition shows:  Both the b^3 and the d^3 are engraving errors; if Beethoven had intended the d^3, he would have had to make it the first note of the measure (2nd 16th).

46

1) May be played as approximately 6 quarter-beats:

INTRODUZIONE.
Adagio molto.

RONDO.

Allegretto moderato.

Attacca subito il Rondo:

1) The intention of Beethoven's long pedals, which take no account of dissonant passing chords or mixtures, is a spiritual, almost transcendental, binding-together of larger groups, which his instrument also favored (cf. Op. 31, No. 2, first movement, mm. 143–148 & 153–158). On modern instruments one may try to achieve this effect by half-pedaling at the passing harmonies (mm. 3, 7, 11, 15, etc.), a kind of legatissimo of the pedal, comparable to legato playing in general.
2) The *pp* at G_1 serves to identify the opening of the motif. 3) Thus in the original edition; some later ones give g^3 in place of f^3.

1) The first 16th note is detached to identify the opening of the motif. 2) Trill starting with the upper note in 32nds. 3) As Beethoven indicates at mm. 490 ff., the trill starting with the upper note is to be played uninterruptedly in 32nds; the fingering given makes this easy to execute.

51

1) The two 8th-rests in place of a quarter-rest, and the ❄ directly below the fourth 8th-beat, are based on the original edition.

1) Usual simplification.

1) In the autograph Beethoven wrote: "Those who have too much difficulty with the trill where it occurs along with the Theme, can use the following simplification: or, depending upon the extent of their powers, can double it by playing two of these sextolets to every quarter note in the bass. At any rate it is not important if this trill comes to lose some of its usual speed."

Sonate.

Op. 57.

Dem Grafen Franz von Brunswick gewidmet.

Allegro assai.

23.

1) The pedal indications are Beethoven's. 2) Trill from below, with an anticipation (c^2) inserted into the Nachschlag:
The shortest execution perhaps thus: . 3) In the autograph and original edition (Bureau des Arts, Vienna) the trill has no addition to it; here one might add g^2 as a short appoggiatura. 4) Only the original grouping of the arpeggio fits the musical meaning.

1) etc. 2) Also thus: 3) As at 2).

1) In the autograph and original edition, c^2 instead of fb^2.

1) In this measure and in m. 160 only the written-out simple Nachschlag is permitted, not the form in m. 156 or 162.

1) In the autograph and original edition, no addition to the trill.   2) Cf. the footnote to m. 45.

1) In mm. 204–205 & 206–207 the 16th-note figure on the first and second quarter-beats—over the long halfnotes in the l. h.—represents 3 x 4 sixteenths; with the beginning of the motif in the l. h., each group of six sixteenths forms a unit. Therefore, to reproduce on the last two quarter-beats the figuration of the first two, as printed in many editions, contradicts the musical meaning.

1) This **exact** reproduction of the autograph and original edition from m. 227 to m. 234 excludes a distribution of the music between both hands. The fingering supplied within parentheses is a suggested simplification through use of the l. h.

1) The l. h. below the r. h.

1) Here, as in mm. 60, 64 & 72, the use of the thumb on the upper keys, too, makes the execution easier and more supple.

86

1) The tie clearly in the autograph.

1) In the autograph there is a natural sign before the D in mm. 291 & 295.

SONATE.

Op. 81ª

Das Lebewohl.

Bei der Abreise S. K. Hoheit des verehrten Erzherzogs Rudolph. Wien, am 21. Mai 1809.*

Adagio.

26.

*) "On the departure of H. M. the revered Lerchduke Rudolph. Vienna, May 21, 1809." (The French entered Vienna in 1809.) In opposition to Beethoven's specific instructions, the original edition bears a title he complained of several times: "Sonate caractéristique: Les adieux, l'absence, et le retour" (The Farewell, The Absence, The Return—Das Lebewohl, Abwesenheit, Wiedersehen).

1) The fingering in italics and the pedal indications are Beethoven's.

1) In the autograph there is a *p* here too, in place of the erased ⟩

6 1) The slur here follows the autograph and the original edition in its difference from mm. 23 & 24.

1) Here the slur is once more like mm. 23 & 24, again on the basis of the autograph and original edition.

1) $d^{\sharp}$ in the l. h. chord according to the autograph.

Abwesenheit.
Andante espressivo.
In gehender Bewegung, doch mit Ausdruck.

1) Execute the ornament (*prallender Doppelschlag*) before the second 8th-beat.
2) Execute the ornament on the fourth 32nd-beat.
3) Beethoven was obviously thinking of a *prallender Doppelschlag* ornamented in trill-like fashion:

Wiedersehen.

Vivacissimamente.
Im lebhaftesten Zeitmaasse.

1) Trill with the Nachschlag bb^1 c^2.

END OF EDITION